RELIEF PITCHERS

Doug Marx

The Rourke Corporation, Inc.
Vero Beach, Florida 32964

Copyright 1991 by The Rourke Corporation, Inc.

All rights reserved. No part of this book may be reproduced or utilized in any form or by any means, electronic or mechanical, including photocopying, recording or by any information storage and retrieval system without permission in writing from the publisher.

The Rourke Corporation, Inc.
P.O. Box 3328, Vero Beach, FL 32964

Marx, Doug.
    Relief pitchers / by Doug Marx.
      p. cm. — (Baseball heroes)
    Includes bibliographical references and index.
    Summary: An explanation and history of relief pitching, with profiles of some of the great performers of this glamorous position, called "firemen."
    ISBN 0-86593-131-3
      1. Pitchers (Baseball)—United States—Biography—Juvenile literature. [1. Pitchers (Baseball) 2. Baseball players.] I. Title. II. Series.
GV865.A1M334   1991
796.357'092'2—dc20   91-2871
    [B]   CIP
                                                                   AC

Series Editor: Gregory Lee
Editor: Marguerite Aronowitz
Book design and production: The Creative Spark, Capistrano Beach, CA
Cover photograph: Dave Stock/ALLSPORT USA
Consultant: Zak Colandrea

Contents

The Bullpen	5
World Series Firemen	13
Changing The Game	21
Judging Relief Pitchers	27
Today's Stars	33
Glossary	42
Bibliography	44
Index	46

Why are there relief pitchers? If your starter tires, you need a "fireman" to come to your team's rescue.

The Bullpen

Imagine you are a relief pitcher. You spend most of your time watching the game from the worst seat in the ballpark. It is called the bullpen. A team's bullpen is usually located at the far ends of the field—in its left and right field corners. It can get lonely and boring out there. It is where a relief pitcher warms up, getting his arm loose before coming into the game.

There you are in the bullpen, "riding the pines" or "catching splinters," which is baseball talk for sitting on the bench. Except for a brief warm-up last inning, you've spent most of the game joking with your teammates: two catchers and three or four other firemen. Firemen

The reliever's reward for a job well done.

Hoyt Wilhelm—the first star reliever in the major leagues—shows off his knuckleball grip.

are relief pitchers. They are expected to come into the game at any time and put out the fire of the opposing team's rally. Now the bullpen telephone is ringing. Your manager tells you to get ready. You start warming up.

Your team is leading 1-0 in the bottom of the ninth. Your pitcher has thrown eight strong innings of shutout ball, but he is starting to tire. The first batter hits a hard drive to deep center field, but it is caught for out number one. It looks like you'll be going in. You start throwing harder, throwing "smoke." Meanwhile, the second batter singles, and the third batter doubles. Suddenly the tying and winning runs are in scoring position. When the fourth man to the plate rips a line shot right at the first baseman for out number two, the manager comes out on the field. He can't take a chance. His pitcher lost his stuff. Taking the ball from him, he gives him a pat of encouragement and sends him to the showers. He waves you in.

You jog toward the pitcher's mound into a tense situation. The next hitter is a powerhouse. He leads the league in home runs, batting average and "ribbies," or runs batted in (RBIs). He does not strike out a lot. The outcome of the entire game is now a duel between you and him.

Taking your warm-up throws, you are at the very center of the game. For the last two hours you have watched it from afar. Now, you are the focus of its most dramatic moment. Pressure situations are your specialty. You do not have time to worry about getting into the game's rhythm. Your team needs just one out to win—right now—and you are determined to get it.

You peer in for the catcher's first signal. . . .

It is easy to see why the relief pitcher has become one of the more glamorous positions in baseball. A hundred years ago, relievers were unheard of. Fifty years ago, they were usually the weaker pitchers who could not make the starting rotation. Today, the strength of a team's bullpen is as important as its starters. In fact, the modern-day appearance of the fireman has changed the game more than any other development.

A Little History

It took a long time for baseball managers to realize that two or three good pitchers per game are better than only one. There's no single reason for this. They just didn't think of it. In a way, they didn't have to.

From baseball's earliest days, right up to the 1950s, relief pitchers were bench-sitters. Starting pitchers were expected to throw a complete nine innings, and did so routinely. Cy Young, Walter Johnson, Christy Mathewson, and other Hall of Fame pitchers threw every three days over long careers. Magnificent athletes, they dominated the game in the early 1900s, and they threw smoke. With pitchers like these, who needed a fireman? Flamethrower Cy Young, who played from 1890 to 1911, leads everyone in lifetime complete games, or CGs, with 749. This is truly a record no modern-era pitcher will ever break.

In Young's day, relief pitchers were the "weeny arms" who sat in the bullpen. For the next 50 years, whenever hitters knocked a starting pitcher out of the game, they knew they could clean up on the relievers. Relief pitchers were used sparingly . In 1904, John McGraw, manager of the world champion New York Giants, called on his relievers a whopping 14 times out of a 162-game season! These days, some major league teams never get that many complete games from their entire staff.

Then, in 1952, everything changed when the New York Giants signed a 28-year-old rookie named Hoyt Wilhelm. He led the league that year in appearances (71) and earned run average (2.34), winning 15 games in relief. Wilhelm's appearance eventually changed baseball as much as did Babe Ruth's home-run derbies of the 1920s.

Hoyt Wilhelm

Wilhelm did not invent the knuckleball, but he perfected it, made it popular, and seldom threw anything else. One pitch after another, this right-hander's knuckleballs would dart and dip and zig-zag, frustrating hitters. Compared to a 95-mile-per-hour fastball, a 60-mile-per-hour knuckler can look pretty tempting to a hitter—until it changes direction like a butterfly.

Wilhelm's favorite pitch jumped around so much that catcher Gus Triandos started using a mitt the size of a pillow to handle it! Wilhelm's knuckleballs broke all records for wild pitches. Eventually playing for nine teams in both leagues, he retired with an all-time lifetime record for game appearances: 1,070.

Despite his many appearances, Wilhelm never led the league in saves, although his 123 wins in relief is still a major league record. Wilhelm was inducted into baseball's Hall of Fame in Cooperstown, New York, in 1985—the first relief pitcher to be so honored.

Elroy Face

Elroy Face joined the Pittsburgh Pirates in 1953, one year after Wilhelm joined the National League Giants. An average reliever for several years, Face came into his own in 1959 when he won an amazing 19 games in relief. A year later he went 10-8 with 24 saves. He saved three games in the Pirates' defeat of the Yankees in the classic 1960 World Series.

Like Wilhelm, Face relied on a special pitch. In 1959, he taught himself how to throw a forkball. Jealous pitchers call it a "freakball," because it takes large hands to hold it. The ball is wedged between the index and middle fingers, and cushioned into the palm. At times Face's forkball seemed unhittable. He used it as an off-speed pitch that sank at the last moment, causing batters to hit a lot of ground balls.

The forkball of Roy Face brought down many a hitter in the late innings of a crucial game—including three saves in the 1960 World Series.

In the 1980s, the forkball became a favorite weapon among pitchers. Face will probably be best remembered for his forkball. The batters all knew it was coming, but they still couldn't hit it.

Once Wilhelm demonstrated the importance of relief pitching, firemen began to appear in growing numbers. Through the '60s and early '70s, many relievers became well-known to fans. Luis Arroyo, Lindy McDaniel, Ron Perranoski, Dick Radatz and Mike Marshall are just five among many ace firemen who entered the record books with season-high saves.

Firemen have become not only numerous and popular, but heroes as well. Tug McGraw, Sparky Lyle, Steve Bedrosian, and Dave Smith are as well-known today as big-time starters like Roger Clemens and Dave Stewart. The number and status of these hurlers pales by comparison to the way they have changed the game. On the field or in the record books, today's baseball can be described as the "Age of the Relief Pitcher."

Before he became a Cy Young-winning starter, Bob Welch was a bullpen ace for the Los Angeles Dodgers.

World Series Firemen

Sparky Lyle was one of the premier firemen of the 1970s. A lefty with a good fastball and better slider, he won 99 games in relief and saved 238. He pitched in 899 games over 16 seasons—every one in relief.

The importance of having an ace fireman in the bullpen can be seen in Lyle's 1976-77 seasons with the Yankees. In 1976, for example, with a league-leading 23 saves and a 2.25 ERA, Lyle helped the Yanks gain a World Series berth. In 1977 his pitching again carried the Yanks into the Series. Down two games to one in the American

Randy Myers saved Game 4 of the 1990 World Series for the Reds.

13

Left-hander Sparky Lyle's best season included saves in the Yankee's 1977 championship wins over the Royals and the Dodgers.

League playoffs against the Royals, Lyle threw 5-2/3 innings of shutout relief in Game Four to even the series. In Game Five he threw another 1-1/3 innings of shutout relief, as the Yankees took the pennant. Two days later, his 3-1/3 innings of one-hit pitching gave the Yankees the World Series opener against the Dodgers. 1977 proved to be Lyle's finest season. Finishing 13-5 with 26 saves, he became the second fireman to win the prestigious Cy Young Award (Mike Marshall was the first relief winner).

One of the game's great clowns, Lyle was well-known for his locker room pranks. Once he jumped naked onto a birthday cake, not knowing it was a present for his manager, Ralph Houk!

Frank "Tug" McGraw

About the same time that Sparky Lyle was the ruling American League fireman, his National League counterpart was Tug McGraw. McGraw was not quite the pitcher that Lyle was, but he was certainly his equal in the clubhouse. A graduate of barber school, McGraw reported to the Mets with a handlebar mustache and shoulder-length hair. One season he even grew tomatoes in the bullpen!

When he was not playing class clown, McGraw got serious with his master pitch, the screwball. Also known as the inshoot, indrop, whisker-trimmer and fadeaway, a screwball is like a reverse curve. It breaks in the opposite direction. For example, a right hander's scroogie will break in toward a right-handed batter around the knees, instead of hitting the outside corner of the plate.

Although McGraw saw little post-season action in the famous "Miracle Mets" World Series victory of 1969, his 9-3 record, with 12 saves, helped get them there. In 1980 he helped the Phillies beat the Royals, closing Games One and Six, losing Game Three, and then winning Game Five. Perhaps more important, McGraw's colorful play and spirit kept his teams going in tough times. "You gotta believe!" he cried, time and again. Eventually the Mets and Phillies made believers out of everyone.

Rich "Goose" Gossage

After six years with the White Sox and the Pirates, Goose Gossage joined the Yankees in 1978, finishing the

Tug McGraw and his screwball helped the New York Mets capture their "miracle" World Series victory of 1969.

year with a 10-11 record and a league-leading 27 saves. Over the next 11 years he became, for many fans, the greatest relief pitcher ever to take the mound.

The heyday years for Gossage were from 1975 to 1986. Big, powerful and mustachioed, Gossage put fear into hitters' hearts first by staring at them, then letting loose with his 100-mile-per-hour fastball. Purely a "short" reliever, Gossage was unhittable in the late innings. George Brett once said of Goose: "There is no one else who can come in and get out of a bases loaded jam with strikeouts like Gossage can."

Growing up in rural areas, Gossage used to spend

hours throwing anything he could get his hands on—rocks, mostly. Later, he would go to the park and throw baseballs at anyone who could catch him. The practice paid off. Although he glowered at the hitters, once he went into his windup, Gossage never looked at the plate. This scared hitters. All arms and legs, twisted up like a pretzel and with his back to the plate, Gossage hid the ball from the hitter until BOOM!—it thundered past the batter and into the catcher's mitt.

By 1988, playing with the Cubs, Gossage had averaged just about one strikeout for every inning he pitched. With a career of 110 wins, 302 saves and a 2.92 ERA, the Goose is still considered one of the best.

Roland "Rollie" Fingers

In January 1991, Rollie Fingers came up 42 votes short in the Hall of Fame balloting. This oversight angered at least one sportswriter, who put his views in print. "Shame on [you]," said Dave Anderson of the *New York Times*, speaking to his fellow sportswriters. "Relief pitchers continue to be the most ignored of the Hall of Fame candidates," he complained.

In his 17-year career, Fingers saved a record 341 games, winning 114 games along the way. His greatest moments came during the early '70s when he was the principal stopper for the powerhouse Oakland A's. During that time, the A's won five division titles, three pennants, and three World Series. In 1974, as the A's dumped the Dodgers four games to one, Fingers saw action in four of the games, winning one and saving two. He received the Series Most Valuable Player (MVP) award for his efforts. Seven years later he won both the American League Cy Young and MVP awards.

Known for his handlebar mustache, Fingers was a

Rich Gossage didn't earn the nickname "Goose" for his pitching.

hard-throwing fireman who had a slider that baffled hitters. This is one of the things that makes Fingers' stats so amazing. Not many fireballers can last 17 seasons, and the slider puts more stress on a pitcher's arm than any other pitch. By no means junk, a slider is a fast, quick curve that does not break until it is on top of the hitter.

Putting together one strong season after another, Fingers proved that hard-throwing relievers could last. Perhaps in the years to come, Hall of Fame voters will recognize Fingers' contribution to baseball and give him the spot in Cooperstown that he deserves.

In 1990 Bobby Thigpen set a new season record for games saved with 57.

Changing The Game

Before firemen came into their own, baseball had two major eras. The first is known as the deadball era. The second is called the liveball, or "modern era." During the deadball era, the game was dominated by pitchers. During the liveball era, hitters such as Lou Gehrig and Hank Aaron became the game's big stars. In the '50s, more than 1,100 home runs per season were hit in the National League. It was common for team batting averages to go well over .300. Today, a high team batting average is about .275.

The emergence of firemen has made baseball more equal between hitters and pitchers. Neither dominates. Superior hitters square off against superior pitchers, and the result is a more thrilling, competitive style of play.

Relief pitching has made life more difficult for hitters in at least two ways. First, a hitter is nearly always going to be facing a strong pitcher at the top of his form. When a pitcher's arm tires, a new, fresh pitcher is brought in. These days, hitters seldom see fat pitches thrown by rag arms.

Second, hitters also must deal with a new pitcher's rhythm and style. After looking at nothing but fastballs for six innings, it's hard to come up against a slow-curve artist who throws a lot of junk. Junk is any off-speed

The bullpen at Dodger Stadium is where relievers warm up in case their arms are needed to finish the game.

pitch: changeups, curves, knuckleballs. After hitting against an overhand flamethrower, for example, it is tough to adjust to a sidearm forkballer. Today a batter will usually see two, if not three or more, pitchers per game. Now there are even "long" and "short" relief pitchers. They are called set-up pitchers and used for three or four innings in the middle of a game. They set the stage for the closer to wrap things up.

   The increased use of firemen has also changed the pitching game. Complete games are almost a thing of the past. Also rare are 30-game winners. This is due both to fewer starts per season and to relief pitchers. A starting pitcher will often leave the game with the score tied, or down by a run. Win or lose, the decision will go to the fireman. Starting pitchers also do not have to pace themselves as much because they know there will be someone to relieve them if they get tired. They can throw as hard as they can for a full five innings without having to worry about the late innings.

Modern Strategy

Another example of the way the fireman has changed the game is today's strategy. Modern managers often play for a small lead, then bring in "the heat"— their relief. This is also why late-inning, come-from-behind games are now so rare. In the old days, relief pitchers were usually brought in after a starter had been routed. Now a manager might bring in a fireman at the first sign of trouble, especially if his bullpen is deep with talent.

The wide use of relief pitchers gives managers a lot to think about. One of the toughest decisions a manager must face is exactly when to change pitchers. Sometimes all this strategy can look silly. For example, think of the times you have seen one manager switch pitchers, then the other manager switch batters, then the other manager switch pitchers, and so on!

Finally, and perhaps best of all, firemen tend to be odd characters. They bring both comic and pitching relief to the game. The baseball term for a clownish, eccentric player is "flake." There tend to be a lot of flakes in the bullpen.

Apart from their personalities, firemen can be a bit flaky as pitchers, too. They tend to be "one-pitch" aces, and they bring an arsenal of new pitches along with them. They throw knuckleballs, forkballs, floaters, butterfly balls, screwballs, and even palm balls. Some

The hard-throwing Rollie Fingers was part of the Oakland A's attack during the mid-1970s.

have funny deliveries, like Dan Quisenberry's submarine-style. Al Hrabosky snarled, growled and stormed around the mound like Hulk Hogan. Rich "Goose" Gossage just stared the hitters down, reared back and threw fastball after fastball, daring anyone to see the ball, much less hit it.

Quirky and tough to hit, relief pitchers have changed the game in every way. They have gone from the bottom of the team roster to the top. In a way, they've made baseball a ten-person game.

The split-fingered fastball was the weapon of star reliever Bruce Sutter.

Judging Relief Pitchers

Modern-era relief pitchers have made record-keeping next to impossible. The statistics that once helped judge a pitcher's strength are no longer very useful. Relief pitching has even made scoring wins a headache. For example, a starter goes five full innings and leaves with a 1-0 lead. Then the fireman comes in and throws "goose eggs," or shutout ball, for the final four innings. Should the starter really get full credit for the win?

Saves, too, is a misleading statistic. A save really loses its meaning when the score is 10-0 in the eighth inning, and a manager brings in a fireman to save his starter's arm. Some fans claim that managers do this just to increase a star fireman's saves. Are saves too cheap, too easy to earn, and therefore meaningless?

The earned run average has also become suspect. For years, the ERA has been a solid measure of a pitcher's quality. A low ERA meant a good pitcher. A good pitcher on a weak-hitting team could lose a lot of ballgames by scores of 2-1 or 3-2. Still, if his ERA was low, we know the losses were not his fault.

Today, just like his win-loss record, a pitcher's ERA is no longer determined by his play alone. If a pitcher leaves the game with the bases loaded and the fireman gives up a grand-slam homer, three of those four runs are charged to the pitcher taking a shower.

Who knows? Maybe that pitcher would have popped up the hitter instead.

And what about the set-up relievers? Although they might pitch more innings than closers, they seldom have a chance to earn either saves or wins.

Some fans have decided that one method of measuring a fireman's talent is to count relief points. Relief points are the sum of a fireman's saves added to his wins. Rollie Fingers leads all firemen in this category. His lifetime 114 wins in relief, plus his record-setting 341 saves, gives him 455 relief points.

But even the idea of a fireman receiving a win for his efforts can often seem silly. Most of the time, a relief pitcher can only win a game if he first loses it. How? Many a reliever's wins come about because he fails to protect the lead in the first place. In other words, if the other team ties the game or goes ahead, then the reliever can earn a win if his team comes from behind.

It is possible that in the future someone will come up with a whole new statistical way of judging pitchers.

Bruce Sutter

Sutter was one of the finest firemen in major league history. During his 12-year career he led the National League in saves five times and finished with 300 lifetime saves. Behind Fingers and Gossage, Sutter is third in career saves. In 1979, while playing for the Cubs, his six wins and 37 saves earned him a Cy Young Award. One of only five relief pitchers to win this award, Sutter did it while playing on a team that did not even make it to the playoffs.

Perhaps more than his superb stats, Sutter will be best remembered as the pitcher who revived Elroy Face's famous forkball by turning it into a split-fingered

The split-fingered fastball is a grip that relievers practice even when they are not throwing.

fastball. The split-fingered fastball has become the most popular pitch in today's game. Everybody is learning how to throw it, and hitters hate it. Sutter started throwing this former junkball with a strong wrist snap and the motion of a fastball. He could make it break either like a curve or a screwball. As his playing days were coming to a close, Sutter threw his "jewel" strikeout pitch 90 percent of the time.

Dan Quisenberry

At the same time Bruce Sutter dominated the National League, Dan Quisenberry ruled supreme in the American League. Playing for the Royals from 1979 to 1988, "Quis" led the league in saves five times, and was one of the main reasons behind the Royals' success as contenders. With 45 and 44 saves in 1983 and '84, many

The "submarine" ball of Dan Quisenberry kept umpires, catchers, batters and fans dizzy just looking at his delivery.

think of him as the fireman of the '80s.

But, it is Quisenberry's style—rather than his stats—that people think of when his name is mentioned. Quis throws a submarine ball. Going into his windup, he twists and bends down so that the ball comes within five or six inches of the mound before its release. It's like throwing underhanded. Quisenberry is not a flamethrower. His best submarine pitch is an 80-mile-per-hour sinker that produces a lot of ground-ball outs. He has perfect control, and he throws a lot of junk along with his sinker.

But as with so many other famous firemen, it is not Quisenberry's talent that teammates and sportswriters love to talk about. It's his personality. Quisenberry is another goofball. Quick-witted, he once said of his submarine motion, "I found a delivery in my flaw." Another Quisenberry line goes like this: "I have seen the future. It is much like the present, only longer." No doubt many hitters have wished that when it comes to Quisenberry, his future be shorter—a lot shorter.

Bullpen Flakes and High Jinx

In their superb book *The Pitcher*, John Thorn and John Holway tell about a reliever named John Stanhouse. Stanhouse played for the Orioles and would occasionally "hang upside down in the bullpen to get a new perspective on the game." His career ended one day when he fell on his head.

What goes on in a fireman's head? There have been some all-time flaky starters, too, but all that sitting around in the bullpen can do funny things to a person. Tug McGraw grew vegetables. He also sat on flagpoles. Whenever Ken Brett got the call to pitch, he would prance and run zigzagging onto the field, as if he were playing horsey. Marty Pattin, who could talk like Donald Duck, would bring his barbecue grill to the games and char up a few steaks. Moe Drabowsky's favorite prank was giving the hot-foot to his bullpen cronies. He once put a five-foot boa constrictor in a teammate's locker.

Writing in *Sports Illustrated*, Dan Quisenberry says that "entertainment" is real important in the bullpen. That entertainment can come in the form of "music, dancing, games or bugs." Some firemen like to play MTV and boogie when their favorite song comes over the ballpark loudspeakers. Others play lawn darts with the long pins that are used to hold the rain-tarp down. A popular sport in all bullpens is to spit sunflower seeds, playing a game similar to pitching pennies.

Thanks to the firemen, the game is just not what it used to be.

Dave Righetti was an excellent starting pitcher when the Yankees decided they needed him more in the bullpen. He was traded in 1990 to the San Francisco Giants.

Today's Stars

Dave Righetti is a rare breed among today's relievers. He signed on with the Yankees as a starter in 1979, winning 33 games and losing 23 in his first four seasons. Moreover, he won the Rookie of the Year award his first season out. When Goose Gossage left the Yankees in 1984, management moved Righetti to the bullpen. He promptly racked up 31 saves. Two years later, he went 8-8 on the year, posting 46 saves. This was a season-high major league record until 1990. From 1984 through 1990 he's had seven seasons in a row with 25 or more saves.

Fans and sportswriters still ask whether Righetti could be better employed as a starter. Righetti himself was troubled by the switch. He felt he still had five or six 20-game seasons in him as a starter. Still, always a team player, he took the move to the bullpen without complaint.

Despite his fine stats pitching in relief, Righetti took a lot of abuse from Yankee fans. The Yankee teams of the '80s were known for a lot of player problems and clubhouse feuding. Righetti, however, never entered into these squabbles. His lifelong dream was to wear Yankee pinstripes. He is the kind of player who signs autographs and personally answers fan mail.

In 1990, Righetti was traded to the San Francisco Giants, where he will no doubt pitch more great innings as a star reliever.

Dennis Eckersley

As a starting pitcher for the Indians, Red Sox and Cubs, Dennis Eckersley posted a 151-128 win-loss record from 1975 to 1986. Moving to the A's in 1987, he became their bullpen stopper, saving 16 games that year. And he had a league-leading 45 saves the next season.

Eckersley led the A's to their 1988 pennant, throwing six shutout innings in playoff action, and earning four saves. As it happened, the World Series proved to be a different story, with "Eck" giving up two runs to the Dodgers in the bottom of the ninth—two runs that cost the A's the game.

It is difficult to say how much longer Eckersley will be effective. Many think the A's are the team of the '90s. Eckersley is still their mainstay, with 16 years under his belt. He might pitch well for a few more years. If he had not made the switch to relief, chances are he would have retired in 1987. With Eckersley leading the way as a fireman, it is quite possible that some of today's leading starters could extend their careers by several years by moving to the bullpen.

Jeff Reardon

If there is any doubt about the importance of relief pitchers in today's game, it disappears when you think of Jeff Reardon.

In 1986 the Minnesota Twins was a club without a bullpen stopper or a future. In 1987, with talent like Kirby Puckett and Gary Gaetti, the Twins finally won their first division championship in 17 years. Jeff "The Terminator" Reardon made the difference. He proved to be the bullpen ace everyone from the fans to the front office had hoped for. He is the only active reliever to

Dennis Eckersley pitched over 10 years as a starter before moving up to a senior post in the Oakland A's bullpen.

The "Terminator"—Jeff Reardon, the major leagues' leader in career saves during the late 1980s.

have 20 or more saves in six straight seasons. From 1988 to 1990 he racked up 107 saves, which is more than any other pitcher.

Reardon is all fireman. He loves "clutch situations," tight spots when the game is on the line. With 287 lifetime saves, he has a good chance of breaking Rollie Fingers' record 341.

Like many relievers, Reardon has his quirk. He carries a lead ball about the size of a softball around with him when he is on the field. The other players "razz" or tease him about this, as if the ball were his pet or teddy bear. Reardon does not mind. When it is time to take the mound, the baseball feels light as a feather. And the hitter's bat feels like a ton of lead.

One reliever to watch in the 1990s is Todd Worrell.

The Up-And-Comers

For every active bullpen ace mentioned in this book, there are at least two others who deserve equal attention. In the '80s, for example, three firemen won the Cy Young Award. Rollie Fingers was one. In 1984, Willie Hernandez went 9-3 and collected 32 saves, posting a 1.93 ERA. Hernandez was also awarded the American League MVP.

A minor-league starter named Steve Bedrosian joined the Braves in 1981, and was promptly converted into a set-up man. He soon became a late-inning closer, but was called on so much that his arm gave out three years later. Traded to Philadelphia, Bedrosian settled into a rhythm that produced 29 saves in 1986 and a league-leading 40 in 1987. For a season that included a record-setting 13 consecutive saves, he won the Cy Young Award.

Eleven-year veteran flamethrower Lee Smith first caught fire with the Cubs, saving a league-leading 29 games in 1983. He has averaged almost 30 saves per season ever since, despite some nagging injuries. At six-feet, six-inches and 245 pounds, the right-hander has been clocked at 101 miles per hour. Traded to the Cardinals in 1990, it looks like he's found a home in St. Louis.

When the Cardinals called up Todd Worrell from the minors late in the 1985 season, he turned in three wins and five saves. Guess who won the pennant? St. Louis. The next year Worrell led the league with 36 saves. Since he continues to have nothing but 30-plus seasons, some fans think Worrell might turn in a 40- or even a 50-save season in the '90s.

John Franco, one of the National League's finest

Dave Smith is climbing fast on the all-time saves list, passing Roy Face in 1990.

The phone rings in the bullpen—it's time to send in the fireman.

relievers, is a change-up artist. In 1990 Franco helped carry the Mets into the pennant race with a league-leading 33 saves. Unfortunately, the Mets' hopes faded as Franco fell out of form in the last three weeks. In his last nine appearances he failed to do the job. No doubt Franco will come back strong as ever. His bad luck was his team's bad luck, which again shows the importance of good relief.

    These are but a few of the relief pitchers who will continue to change baseball through the '90s. Others to watch are Bobby Thigpen, Dave Smith and Lance McCullers. If they improve like the firemen of the '70s and '80s, we might see a completely different approach to pitching by the year 2000. Who knows—as relievers dominate the game more and more, maybe the whole idea of a "starting" pitcher will vanish. Some fans think the "Age of the Relief Pitcher" has yet to begin.

Glossary

BULLPEN. Tradition has it that the word comes from advertising. In the old days, the Bull Durham Tobacco Company had a lot of signboards in big league ballparks. Some of them were posted where the relief pitchers and second-string catchers were stationed, far down the outfield lines. Most of the time they chewed Bull Durham tobacco and "shot the bull."

CLOSER. A relief pitcher who is brought in only in the late innings. His special function is to "close" the game, to protect the lead and wrap things up.

DEADBALL. In the early days of baseball, the ball did not travel as well when hit.

FASTBALL. A pitch straight into the strike zone.

FAT PITCHES. A pitch that is easy to hit.

FIREMAN. A relief pitcher. The nickname comes from the fact that relievers are brought in to stop a rally, or put out the other team's fire.

FORKBALL. See split-finger fastball.

JUNK. Off-speed pitches. Curveballs, forkballs, knuckleballs and changeups are all off-speed. The word was probably coined by a frustrated hitter who struck out, wrenching his back on a slow curve.

KNUCKLEBALL. An off-speed pitch thrown with the fingertips.

LIVEBALL. Today's baseball with a cork center that flies farther when hit.

RAG ARMS. When a pitcher's arm tires in the later innings of a game.

RELIEF POINTS. The fan's preferred scoring method for relief pitchers.

SCREWBALL. An off-speed pitch thrown by turning the wrist inward.

SET-UP PITCHERS. Relief pitchers who specialize in pitching the middle innings of a game.

SLIDER. A fast curveball that breaks downward abruptly underneath the batter's swing.

SPLIT-FINGER FASTBALL. A pitch thrown using the index and middle fingers, cushioned in the palm. This is a difficult pitch to learn, and one of the most popular in today's pro game.

STOPPER. A relief pitcher, a fireman, a closer—the hurler who comes in to stop the other team from scoring.

Bibliography

Books

Angell, Roger. *Season Ticket.* Boston: Houghton Mifflin, 1988.

Durant, John. *The Story of Baseball in Words and Pictures.* New York: Hastings House, 1973.

James, Bill. *The Bill James Historical Baseball Abstract.* New York: Villard Books, 1986.

Laird, A.W. *Ranking Baseball's Elite.* Jefferson, North Carolina: McFarland & Company, Inc., Publishers, 1990.

Thorn, John, and Pete Palmer. *Total Baseball.* New York: Warner Books, 1989.

Thorn, John, and John Holway. *The Pitcher.* New York: Prentice Hall Press, 1987.

Periodicals

Gammons, Peter, and Robert W. Creamer. "How Do You Spell Success? R-E-L-I-E-F." *Sports Illustrated.* April 4, 1988: 76-78.

Lieber, Jill. "The Relief Is Not So Sweet." *Sports Illustrated.* April 16, 1990: 70-73.

Quisenberry, Dan. "The Land of Stupid Dances." *Sports Illustrated.* April 16, 1990: 56-59.

Ruesse, Patrick. "Reardon Lets the Good Times Roll." *The Sporting News.* October 12, 1987: 14-15.

Sexton, Joe. "At Home, Met Hero Has Arm of Clay." *The New York Times.* February 4, 1990: B11.

Wulf, Steve. "The Big Sweep." *Sports Illustrated.* October 29, 1990: 18.

Index

Arroyo, Luis, 11

Bedrosian, Steve, 11, 38
Brett, Ken, 31

Drabowsky, Moe, 31

Eckersley, Dennis, 34

Face, Elroy, 9-11, 28
fastball, 16
Fingers, Roland ("Rollie"), 17-19, 28, 36
forkball, 9-11, 28
Franco, John, 38-40

Gossage, Rich ("Goose"), 15-17, 25, 33

Hernandez, Willie, 38
Hrabosky, Al, 25

Johnson, Walter, 8

knuckleball, 8-9

Lyle, Sparky, 11, 13-15

Marshall, Mike, 11
Mathewson, Christy, 8
McCullers, Lance, 40
McDaniel, Lindy, 11
McGraw, Frank ("Tug"), 11, 15, 31

off-speed pitches, 21-22

Pattin, Marty, 31
Perranoski, Ron, 11

Quisenberry, Dan, 25, 29-31

Radatz, Dick, 11
Reardon, Jeff, 34

relievers
    and earned run average (ERA), 27
    and relief points, 28
    and saves, 27
    and strategy, 21-25
    judging of, 27-28
    most saves (career), 17
    most saves (season), 33
Righetti, Dave 33

screwball, 15
slider, 17-19
Smith, Dave, 11, 40
Smith, Lee, 38
split-fingered fastball, 29
Stanhouse, John, 31
submarine ball, 30-31
Sutter, Bruce, 28-29

Thigpen, Bobby, 40

Wilhelm, Hoyt, 8-9
Worrell, Todd, 38

Young, Cy, 8
Young Award, Cy, 14, 17, 28, 38

About The Author

Doug Marx is a 41-year-old poet and freelance writer who, when not reading books or writing them, suffers from "baseball on the brain." Having played at the little league, high school and college levels, he now plays a hot third base for the Grass Stains, a men's softball team. Marx, who spent the better part of his childhood bouncing rubber-coated hardballs off brick walls, has also spent many years coaching boys' and girls' little league teams. He lives in Portland, Oregon, with his wife and three children.

Picture Credits

ALLSPORT USA: 4 (J. Rettaliata); 5, 39 (Kirk Schlea); 12 (Robert Beck); 13, 35, 36 (Otto Greule, Jr.); 20 (Tim DeFrisco); 26 (John Swart); 30 (Don Smith); 32 (T.G. Higgins); 37 (ALLSPORT)
National Baseball Library, Cooperstown, NY: 6, 10, 14, 16, 18, 24
Sports Illustrated: 22 (Andrew Bernstein); 29 (Bill Smith); 40 (V.J. Lovero)

DATE DUE

MY 12 '98			
MY 19 '98			
MY 27 '98			
OC 09 '98			

Book is marked   5796   MAY 14 1997
                         20075
796.357 Marx, Doug   SE 19 '97
Ma   SE 26 '97
         Relief pitchers OC 08 '97
                          MR 18 '98
                          MR 31 '98
                          AP 24 '98

GUMDROP BOOKS - Bethany, Missouri